Food Truck Business:
How to start your own Food Truck while growing and succeeding as your own boss!

By Fiona Hathaway

Table of Contents

Table of Contents

Copyright

Introduction

I want to thank and congratulate you for downloading the book "*Food Truck Business: How to start your own Food Truck while growing and succeeding as your own boss!*" Food Trucks have slowly become some of the best places for you to get your food from. They're unique, and they can certainly get people's attention easily mainly because of the fact that they're unlike other food businesses in the market.

What's also great about Food Trucks is the fact that it's more manageable than a restaurant, plus it's also something that will set you apart from your contemporaries in the food niche. You can definitely be your own boss, and you can watch your business grow—right in the truck!

So, how exactly can you start your on Food Truck Business?

Well, this book is your complete crash course regarding starting your own Food Truck

Business! From the things that you should do to the questions you have to ask yourself, you'll find them all right here!

What are you waiting for?

Start reading this book now and start your own Food Truck Business as soon as you can!

Once again, thank you and enjoy!

Chapter 1: First, get a License

It's a very basic guideline that before you get on the road and set up your Food Truck business, you have to get a license first. It's one of the non-negotiables when it comes to this kind of business, especially because you really do not want to deal with the authorities asking you why you're parking your truck in an open space with a lot of people around. Remember, a food truck is a business that is situated in a truck and of course, a truck is a vehicle that takes up a lot of space so it's just right that you get a license to make everything legal.

If you're planning to start a business in the coming year, make sure that you file for your license before January as there usually is a long wait list of people who want to obtain licenses in the said month and you certainly wouldn't want to be part of that. Furthermore, you should also check with your local government unit about requirements as they differ from each state.

When you do this, everything will be easy. However, there are a couple of things that are mostly similar when it comes to licenses for food business and these are:

1. Food Manager Identification Card from your district.
2. Proper Identification and Proof of Ownership.
3. Food Record Keeping.
4. Food Storage Record.
5. Business Plan.
6. Copy of a written message of support from your community leaders.

Once you obtain all these and contact your local government units for further information, you're all set to have your license!

So, now that you have a license, you should now get your own truck—and decide what you want to sell!

Chapter 2: Get a Truck

Now, you should be able to get your own truck for your business. You should be ready to shell out around $20,000 to $40,000 for this, plus you should also be ready to cough up some money for the equipment that you will be using. If you feel like it's too expensive, don't fret. If you're really serious about this business, you have to be ready for all these expenses because you should have a truck that will meet the public health standards. As for the equipment, it always differs as it's based on your needs and preferences and on the kind of food business that you have. If you're planning to sell hotdogs, you should have all these frying equipment, as well as containers for condiments and other ingredients. If you're planning to sell pizza, you should have ovens, baking pans, trays, and the like. You can also save money if you're planning to just sell pre-packaged foods already, so mainly you just need to have a lot of containers around.

Also, it would be great if you will decide which kind of food truck business are you going to embark on. This will help you decide which type of equipment you need, and will also help you when it comes to decorating your food truck based on your niche.

Here are some of the types of food trucks that you should know about:

1.   **Mobile Food Preparation Vehicle**. This is a food truck that lets customers order their food and wait for their food to be cooked. Even though that's the case, it's also imperative that you should not let your customers wait for long. It's like your typical fast food restaurant or fast food kiosk, so of course, you expect that your customers are already hungry so it's best that you make them great food and you serve them as soon as you can. They are also called concession trailers.

2.   **Industrial Catering Vehicle.** As the name suggests, this is the kind of truck that

you can take around town, such as those old-school ice cream or hotdog trucks that you see around. Industrial Catering Vehicles mostly sell pre-packaged foods, which makes it more cost-friendly than a Mobile Food Preparation Vehicle. The only catch is that you have to make sure that you're able to sell everything right away or else you'd be throwing away a whole lot of cash because obviously, you can't sell what's already spoiled. Both Industrial Catering and Mobile Food Preparation Vehicles are often found in school fairs, concerts, and other events where there are loads of people around.

3. Gourmet Food Trucks. Imagine eating the best gourmet foods in an unusual setting—that's what gourmet food trucks are all about! Sometimes, you want to eat at a certain restaurant but you can't because you haven't got any reservations. But, because of gourmet food trucks, you'll be able to enjoy the food that you want as they sell specialty foods, such as velvet cupcakes, Korean barbecue, orzo fries, crepes, and even smoothies or other kinds of drinks that can't usually be bought outside. Of course, these food trucks require special equipment so you have to be ready for the fees but if you already get to establish your name in the food truck industry and if you already have a following, it'll be easy for you to earn back your capital. Sometimes, you can also invite well-known chefs to cook for you, or if you're a chef yourself, this can be a good place for you to showcase your cooking prowess!

Decide which type of truck you'd like to use for your business then go on and plan your menu. You'll learn more about this in the next chapter!

Chapter 3: Plan Your Menu

Just like any other food business out there, you definitely shouldn't just go in your truck without knowing what you're going to sell. You have to decide what you want to cook and what you want to sell so that you can be sure that your business will start rolling.

In order to plan the perfect menu, you should ask yourself some questions that will make the business of choosing which foods should go on the menu easy for you. Here are some of those questions:

1. **What's easy for you to cook?** Can you cook hotdogs without burning either side? Can you flip pancakes like a pro? Do you know how to make delicious patties with just the right amount of condiments? You have to determine what you can cook so you can narrow your choices down instead of overwhelming yourself

with the thought that you should cook every dish in the world.

1. **What's your specialty?** Of course, there are a couple of dishes that you know how to cook and that's exactly why you're planning to open a food truck business. But, there will always be a dish that you're confident about and that you know you can cook better than anyone else does. What is it? Think about it and think about how you can use it for this business. For example, you can cook Fettuccine Alfredo like you're from Italy and you know that it tastes different from what others make. Think about that and see if you can make more variations, or if you want to feature the said dish with some side dishes. This way, when people think about your food truck, they'll remember your specialty dish and they'd keep coming back for more.

2. **Which ingredients are easy to get around you?** Maybe, you're planning to put up a hotdog food truck but you're in an area where there's loads of fish and fresh produce around. What do you do? Will you still get meat for the hotdog from another town, or will you make use of the ingredients close to you, especially if you can actually make great dishes out of them? Sometimes, it's important to look around and see what you can do with what you have around you because that will save you a lot of money and may even make you closer to people around you, as well!

3. **What do the people around you love to eat? Or, what are they looking for?** Get to know your customers. Of course, it may be impossible to meet each and every one of them but it wouldn't be impossible to observe and make a general assessment as to what kind of food they enjoy the most. This way, when you

set up your food truck, you can be sure that at least one or two people will try what you have to offer. On the other hand, you can also observe what's lacking in the area and you can check whether you can give them that or not. For example, New York is full of these pizza, pretzel, and hotdog kiosks and food trucks. However, there's a lack of sushi trucks or even trucks that sell ramen or maybe even something organic. You see, there are so many things that you can cook and offer people so research on that. If you offer people what they're missing or what's not currently available in the area, you just might get a positive response because more often than not, people want to try what they still haven't before.

1.   **What kinds of food can customers easily take with them?** As a customer, it's important to know that you'll be able to eat something easy to bring especially because

most people are on the go these days. So, it's essential that you make the packaging of your products efficient so that people won't have a hard time with them.

4. **Which ingredients are too costly?** Think about the dishes that you'll be making and see to it that you're not wasting too much money on ingredients, especially if you don't have enough budget to begin with. Think about a dish that you can make and you know you're good at that won't cost too much. It's important not to waste a lot of money when you're only starting.

5. **Which ingredients are portable?** There may be times when you lack ingredients in the truck and you have to buy some more from the nearest store—but what if it's a couple of miles away? You have to think about the ingredients that you'll be using, too, because they're important when it comes to the dishes that you'll be cooking.

6. **Which food products are easy to re-heat?** If you're planning to set up an Industrial Catering Vehicle, it would be important to know which food products can you easily re-heat without them losing their quality, and you have to learn which foods don't get spoiled easily, as well, as you'll be traveling around a lot.

7. **Will you focus on your expertise, or are you willing to try something new?** Suppose you're famous for creating delicious and appetizing cupcakes. Are you going to sell them or make them the focus of your business? Or are you also willing to learn how to make other dishes and make use of them, too? Diversity is very important when it comes to food trucks, sure, but being confident with what you're doing is also one of the biggest keys to success.

8. **Will your menu always be your menu, or will you be able to change it?** It's important to observe whether your

customers like your menu or not and be open to changes, if needed.

9. **What time will you be open and on which days?** You have to create a schedule and you have to stick to it because when your customers notice that you're not around for a day or two, and when they feel like you're not open at a certain given time, they may think that you're no longer in business or that you're not serious with what you're doing—and that's definitely something that you shouldn't allow to happen.

Then, when you finally decide what kind of menu you'd offer to your customers, you have to make sure that you get to cook the food right and that you think about some guidelines that will help you create the perfect food truck dish for your customers.

These guidelines are:

1. **You have to make sure that you are consistent.** Consistent in what, you ask? Well, consistent when it comes to making good food. Remember that you're not planning to have people eat at your place and never come back anymore, right? So, you have to make sure that you always get to create good food so when they recommend you to other people, they won't be embarrassed that they did so and you'd gain more customers, too.

2. **Make sure that you can cook in large quantities.** Remember, you're not going to serve one person alone, so it's best if you learn how to cook lots of food in a short amount of time. But of course, it's not just quantity that's important, quality is also essential—and will always be essential, so make great food in large numbers and you're all set.

3. **Make food that you won't have a hard time serving.** Food Trucks are mainly created for people who are on the go so you have to learn how to work fast but still make sure that what you're doing is right. Create dishes that are easy to serve so people won't be bored and there won't be more pressure on you.

4. **And, make food that won't spoil even if it's taken on the road.** You have to expect that your customers will take their orders with them on the go. Of course, some people may stay at your food truck and eat but most of the customers may choose to just bring their orders with them. Take care of the packaging and make sure to use only the right kinds of ingredients.

Extras

As time goes by, you can also add more dishes on your menu and you may also add some other items in your truck that you could sell. These items include official merchandise with the name of your business, some souvenirs that customers can give away, and other things that will remind them of your business so that they won't forget it right away. Make sure though that you leave them a good impression so they'd want to buy these extra items.

If you know how to plan your food truck menu, things will definitely be much easier for you!

Chapter 4: The Design

Now that you have a menu, it's also important that you make your truck stand out from the rest. You can do this by means of aesthetics. While some people say that food is the only important thing in any food business, you know for a fact that it isn't true. Of course, it's also important for customers to be able to eat somewhere nice because no one really wants to eat in a truck that's rusty or that's not even designed at all. If you don't have time to set up your truck in such a way that it would attract people, it may also mean that you are not yet ready for this business and that you may have to really think things through.

Anyway, there are some things that you have to keep in mind when it comes to designing and decorating your food truck. These things are:

1.   **The Theme.** Suppose you're creating a burger business. It won't be right to use pastels as the theme or put photos of classic Hollywood

stars on the walls of your truck, would it? You have to make sure that the theme you choose is connected to what you're serving so that your customers won't be confused.

2. **Color Scheme.** The main rule is to use the colors on the opposing sides of the color wheel. This way, everything will go together and your truck won't look like it's painted by a two year old. Also, it would be nice if the color scheme of your truck is also something you can use for the uniforms of you and your staff to make everything cohesive.

3. **Seats.** Some food trucks actually allow their customers to sit around the truck so if you can put out some chairs or anything that your customers can sit on, that would be good.

4. **Utensils and Packaging.** It would also be nice if you could set up the truck in such a way that your customers won't have a hard time getting the utensils that they need. Always keep condiments and tissues around because most customers need them, and make sure

that you have environment-friendly bags that they can just pick up and put their orders in so they can take them on the go.

5.   **And of course, give it some life.** The best thing that you can do with your truck is put some of your personality in it. This way, you're truck won't be generic and when people see it, they'll be excited to eat. When people notice that a food truck has life and that it's something cool, chances are they'll really go on and try your products—and that's something that's definitely good for you!

Attract customers and they certainly will eat what you have prepared! Let your truck speak for itself.

Chapter 5: The Location

Next, you have to choose where you'd like to set up your truck. There are certain areas that attract food truck loyalists more than others and these are those places that you have to target. These are:

1.   **Famous Tourist Destinations.** Why? Well, exactly because you know that people will be flocking around the area! There's definitely a place in your town that people usually frequent and that people from all over the world visit. If you can get a permit to set your truck up there, then you'd be on the right track. And, if this is the case, you might as well sell food that are connected to your area or food that your area is known for so you can be sure that people will try what you have to offer.

2.   **Malls or Shopping Districts.** Again, there are a lot of people around these areas and everyone knows that shopping isn't for

the faint of heart. Sometimes, people go from shop to shop and that's very tiring so of course, they'd get tired and hungry and when the lines are too long in the restaurants at the mall, they'd look for somewhere else to eat—such as your food truck! This way, they can also bond with their family or friends more and have fun choosing orders from your menu!

3.   **Empty Lots.** It's simple: when a lot is empty, there's a lot that you can do with it. Before a restaurant gets built or before people loiter around the area with nothing to do, why don't you get a license and set your truck up there? It's a good way to make money and attract people to try something new instead of just sitting around and doing nothing. Think of the empty lot as an empty mind—it's so open for possibilities and that's what you want your business to have! This way, it'll be easy for people to associate the lot with your food truck and they'll find it as a great place to hang around in.

4.   **Office Parking Lots**. Working at an office is not always easy. There are times when the workload is just too much that one is forced to take back their food to their cubicle with them. In this case, they need to be able to eat somewhere nice and different, just to get away from the monotony of it all, but they also have to make sure that they won't burn a hole in their pockets. As for this, you may want to put up your food truck in an office parking lot so that office workers won't have to go far just to eat lunch or get themselves some snacks. As there are loads of office workers and long office hours, you can be sure that you'll definitely earn a lot! In fact, during lunchtime alone, you'll probably be able to get most of your capital back so this is definitely a good place for you to put your truck in.

5.   **Business Districts.** Don't stick to one office alone—target the whole business district. This way, when people are out of their

offices for an hour or so, they can just check out your food truck and eat something or buy something that they can take with them on the go!

6. **College Campuses.** You know how college kids want to try everything, right? So, of course, when they see a food truck around the campus or even just a couple of blocks away, they'll definitely be rushing to try what you have to offer—which is a good thing for your business. Plus, in this age of social media, they'll surely post photos of your truck and your products online which is a great form of free advertising for you!

7. **Train/Bus Stations.** These are places where people have to wait for their ride and more often than not, they'll be looking for something that they could munch on. So, when they see your food truck, they'll feel as if their prayers have been answered and they'll be thankful that you're there to save them from their misery!

8.   **Beaches.** Not all people have the time to prepare food for beach trips. Sometimes, they just want to go there and of course, it would also be hard if they spend all their money on restaurants around the area as they may be too pricey. But, with your food truck around, they have an alternative to the usual fruits or kebobs and surely, they'll be able to enjoy that.

9.   **Events or Festivals.** Make yourself available and send your plans to event organizers. Chances are, they'll allow you to set up your truck in a certain festival or event because there are a lot of people around and of course, they wouldn't just spend their time listening to the bands, they'd also want something to eat—so you have to be able to give them what they want.

10.   **Sports Events.** If it's an outdoor setting, great. But, if it's an indoor setting, that's okay, too. Just wait for the event to finish, or be there before it starts so while

people are waiting in line, they can order some food from you and they won't just stand there being bored.

Remember, before you park your truck in any of these spaces, make sure that you have the license and that you have talked to the right people so everything will be official and you won't have any problems.

Chapter 6: And, don't forget to market your truck

Marketing is very important in any kind of business.

Basically, if you don't know how to market your business and tell people about it, how can you expect them to check your business out? No one became successful without the help of other people and most importantly, no one became successful without marketing their products or services.

So, how exactly can you market your food truck? Here are some tips:

1. **Get connected.** First, you have to get connected. Stay in touch not just with your family or your close friends, but also with people you have encountered along the way. Keep their contact numbers or e-mail addresses so you could send out some message blasts that will help them know about your endeavors so that hopefully, they will check them out.

2. **Word of mouth.** You know what? Word of mouth is still a foolproof way of being successful in any line of business. If people talk about you and can say something nice about your business to others then more people would check out your business and it's going to be a never-ending cycle of people saying great things about your business to others. So, make sure that you know how to socialize and talk to your customers—or to your potential customers!

3. **Create contests.** Give a free extra burger to the first person who finishes his burger in a certain amount of time. Give free drinks. Give t-shirts or memorabilia as prizes. This is now a growing trend for most food businesses because it keeps people curios about the kind of food that they offer and of course, everybody loves freebies! Everyone loves to win—and that's why you have to give people what they want.

4. **Make online contests.** It's an easier way of gaining buzz and making sure that people will stay tuned for what you have to offer.

It's also a good way of putting the word out about your business.

5.   **Make use of Social Media.** Again, it's the age of social media. Almost everyone has a social media account, whether it's on Facebook, Twitter, or Instagram—and that's why you also have to make an account for your food truck business on these sites. The great thing about social media is that it makes it so easy for you to tell the world about your business. Create a Facebook Fanpage, tweet something about your business, and post photos on Instagram or Pinterest and you're all set. Also, don't forget to create and account on LinkedIn so that you can tell the professional world about you, too! And, don't forget to reply to your followers—it's a very simple thing that most business owners neglect. It's important to create a great relationship with your followers and this is one of the ways of doing so.

Market your business well and it will succeed—not only today but in the long run, too!

Conclusion

Thank you for reading this book!

I hope this book was able to help you understand how you can set up your own food truck business and how you can be successful at it.

Keep the tips given in this book in mind and you'll surely be able to put up the best food truck out there.